AMELIA *Earhart*

SPIRIT
of America®

AMELIA *Earhart*

AVIATION PIONEER

By Cynthia Klingel

*Content Adviser: Louise Foudray, Caretaker and Manager,
Amelia Earhart Birthplace Museum, Atchison, Kansas*

The Child's World

The Child's World®
Chanhassen, Minnesota

6

AMELIA *Earhart*

Published in the United States of America by The Child's World®
PO Box 326 • Chanhassen, MN 55317-0326 • 800-599-READ • www.childsworld.com

Acknowledgments
The Child's World®: Mary Berendes, Publishing Director

Editorial Directions, Inc.: E. Russell Primm, Editorial Director; Pam Rosenberg, Line Editor; Elizabeth K. Martin, Assistant Editor; Olivia Nellums, Editorial Assistant; Susan Hindman, Copy Editor; Susan Ashley, Halley Gatenby, Proofreaders; Jean Cotterell, Kevin Cunningham, Peter Garnham, Fact Checkers; Tim Griffin/IndexServ, Indexer; Dawn Friedman, Photo Researcher; Linda S. Koutris, Photo Selector

Photo
Cover: Bettmann/Corbis; Farwell T. Brown Photographic Archive/Ames (Iowa) Public Library: 15; AP/Wide World Photos: 23, 25, 27; Bettmann/Corbis: 2, /14, 21, 22, 26; Corbis: 9, 28; E.O. Hoppé/Corbis: 18; Underwood & UnderwoodCorbis: 20; Donald E. Martin, Atchison, KS: 10, 11; The Schlesinger Library, Radcliffe Institute, Harvard University: 6, 7 top and bottom, 8, 12, 13, 17; Hulton Archive/Getty Images: 19; Purdue University Libraries' Amelia Earhart Special Collections: 16..

Library of Congress Cataloging-in-Publication Data
Klingel, Cynthia Fitterer.
  Amelia Earhart : aviation pioneer / by Cynthia Klingel.
    p. cm. — (Our people)
Includes index.
  ISBN 1-59296-000-6 (library bound : alk. paper)
  1. Earhart, Amelia, 1897–1937—Juvenile literature. 2. Women air pilots—United States—Biography—Juvenile literature. 3. Air pilots—United States—Biography—Juvenile literature. I. Title. II. Series.
  TL540.E3K54 2004
  629.13'092—dc21   2003004158

14   25   26

Contents

Chapter ONE

Not an Ordinary Gir

Amelia Earhart lived in Atchison, Kansas, when this photo was taken in 1903.

AMELIA EARHART WILL ALWAYS BE KNOWN AS one of America's most famous pilots. She lived at a time when airplane flight was becoming possible. People were fascinated with the pilots who dared to risk their lives in the air.

Amelia was born in Atchison, Kansas, on July 24, 1897. Her father, Edwin Stanton Earhart, was a lawyer. Her mother, Amy Otis Earhart, was from a wealthy family. Amelia's grandfather, Alfred Otis, was a judge and president of the

Atchison Savings Bank. Amelia was born in his large white house on Quality Hill.

At this time in the United States, girls were expected to wear dresses, learn to cook and sew, and behave in a quiet, mannerly way. Most girls weren't encouraged to look for adventure. But Amelia's mother and father loved adventure. In fact, Amelia's mother was the first woman to climb Pikes Peak, a mountain in Colorado. They raised Amelia and her sister, Muriel, in a different way. Amelia and Muriel wore bloomers—a type of pants—instead of dresses. They went fishing and built things with their grandfather's tools.

One time, Amelia saw a roller coaster and decided to build one in their backyard. When she was ten years old,

Amy Otis Earhart and Edwin Stanton Earhart were Amelia Earhart's parents.

Amelia and her sister Muriel on the front porch of their home

her father gave her a gun to shoot the rats in the barn. She rode bicycles and flew down snowy hills on a sled that only boys usually rode. She liked **mechanical** things and once built a trap to catch stray chickens.

Most other girls did not even try to do the things that boys did. But Amelia grew up believing that girls could accomplish the same things as boys. She often cut out magazine articles about careers that most people thought were just for boys.

Amelia, Muriel, and their mother spent a lot of time living with Amelia's grandparents in Atchison. Mr. Earhart's work involved a lot of

Amelia and Muriel liked to play outdoors and try different activities.

8

travel. In 1905, he took a job in Des Moines, Iowa. The girls stayed in Atchison and lived with their grandparents. Three years later, the girls joined their parents in Des Moines. Amelia's father was becoming very successful. Then he began having trouble. He suffered from **alcoholism.** Life for the family was not happy. In 1914, he lost his job. The family moved many times, including to St. Paul, Minnesota, and then Springfield, Missouri, but Mr. Earhart could not get a job. Finally, Mrs. Earhart took the girls and went to Chicago.

Amelia Earhart spent much of her childhood living in Atchison, Kansas, with her mother and grandparents.

Interesting Fact

▸ Amelia was named Amelia Mary Earhart. She was named for her grandmothers, Amelia Otis and Mary Earhart.

9

THE AMELIA EARHART BIRTHPLACE MUSEUM IS LOCATED IN ATCHISON, KANSAS. The museum is actually the former home of Amelia's grandparents, Judge Alfred Otis and Amelia Otis. This is where Amelia Earhart was born. Although her family lived in several places, Amelia considered Atchison to be her hometown. She spent many of her childhood years in her grandparents' home. In 1971, it was added to the National Register of Historic Sites.

The house was built by her grandparents in the 1860s. They lived there until their deaths. From 1912 until 1956, two different families lived in the house. In 1956, it was sold to Paul and Winney Allingham. The Allinghams had no children. In 1984, after their deaths, the house was for sale.

It was purchased by the Ninety-Nines, an organization of women pilots, in 1984. Since then, the group has held fund-raisers to restore and improve the house. The 100th anniversary of Amelia Earhart's birth was in 1997. To celebrate the day, the Kansas Historical Society awarded the Nyle J. Miller Award to the Ninety-Nines for its work in restoring the house.

Thousands of visitors tour Earhart's Birthplace each year. It is located at 223 North Terrace Street in Atchison. You can find more information about the museum at **www.ameliaearhartmuseum.org.**

Chapter TWO

Amelia Takes Flight

Amelia Earhart in 1915, the year before her high school graduation

AMELIA EARHART GRADUATED FROM HYDE PARK High School in Chicago. She attended six high schools over the years because her family moved so often. She worked hard to keep up with her schoolwork so that she would graduate on schedule in 1916. In her high school yearbook, there is a caption with her picture that calls her "the girl in brown who walks alone." Brown was her favorite color, and she was a loner.

By then, Mr. Earhart was recovering from his alcoholism. Amelia, Muriel, and Mrs. Earhart moved to Kansas City to join him.

Soon after, Amelia was sent to the Ogontz School in Rydal, Pennsylvania, to continue her education.

For the Christmas break during her second year at Ogontz, Amelia went to Toronto, Canada. She wanted to visit Muriel, who was attending school there. This visit was important for Amelia's future. While she was there, she saw some men who had been fighting in World War I. Seeing their injuries had a strong effect on her. She decided that she needed to help. She quit school and took a job as a nurse's aide at the Spadina Military Hospital in Toronto.

While at the hospital, she sometimes heard stories of bravery from pilots who had flown in the war. She became interested in airplanes. Then, one day, she went to the

When she was a young woman, Earhart worked for a time as a nurse's aid in the Canadian city of Toronto, Ontario.

Interesting Fact

▸ As a child, Amelia had a big black dog named James Ferocious.

At early air shows, spectators were amazed by the stunts of wing walkers.

Toronto Fair to watch an air show. At this time, airplanes were used for war. They were not used to take people from one place to another for business or vacation. At the air show, stunt pilots flew, spun, and dove through the air. It was very exciting. Amelia wanted to know how the airplane engines worked. She signed up for a course in engine mechanics.

In 1919, Amelia left Toronto. She decided to begin **premedical** classes at Columbia University in New York City. She was a good student. But after one year, she decided to join her mother and father. They were living in California, and she could finish her education there.

It was December 1920. Before she started school again, she and her father visited an air show. At this event, people could actually ride in an airplane. Amelia bought a ticket for a

flight. The next day, she climbed into a plane for the ride that changed her life. Before it was over, she knew that she wanted to be a pilot.

She signed up for flying lessons right away. They were very expensive. Her parents could not afford them. Instead of going back to school, Amelia started working to pay for her lessons. She took her first flying lesson on January 3, 1921. Her teacher was Neta Snook, the first woman to attend the Curtiss School of **Aviation.**

Neta Snook was the instructor who taught Amelia Earhart how to fly.

Interesting Fact

▸ A jointed wooden donkey was Amelia's special toy when she was a child.

15

Amelia Earhart called her first plane the Canary *because it was yellow.*

Within two years, Amelia earned her pilot's license. She became one of the few women in the world who were licensed to fly.

Earhart had to rent an airplane each time she flew. This was expensive, so she took another job to pay for more flying time. In 1922, with financial help from her mother and Muriel, she purchased her first airplane. It was a bright yellow plane that Earhart called the *Canary.* It was so light she could lift its tail to move it. She flew as often as she could. Earhart wanted to know how to control her plane in all possible situations. She practiced dangerous moves. She practiced landing her plane with the engines off. She flew in many different weather conditions.

On October 22, 1922, Earhart set her first flight record. She flew to 14,000 feet (4,267 meters), almost 3 miles (5 kilometers) high. It was the highest a woman had ever flown.

THE NINETY-NINES IS AN ORGANIZATION FOR FEMALE LICENSED PILOTS. IT has about 6,000 members. Most are from the United States, but some are from countries around the world. It is named for the 99 original members of the club.

In 1929, there was a Women's Air **Derby**. It was a race from California to Ohio. Nineteen pilots, including Amelia Earhart, entered the race. When the planes reached Ohio, 20,000 people were there to see the end of the race.

This was the first time woman pilots had gotten together in such a large group. They enjoyed meeting one another. After they went home, many of them thought about getting together again. Letters were sent to the 117 licensed woman pilots in the United States asking them to form an organization.

The response was great—99 women answered. So, on November 2, 1929, the Ninety-Nines was formed. Two years later, members decided they needed a president. Amelia Earhart was elected the first president.

Today, the group still has the same goals as it did 80 years ago—to provide educational opportunities and support for women in aviation and **aerospace**. The group gives workshops for teachers and airline workers, sponsors pilot-safety programs, leads airport tours for children, and holds special classes for people who have a fear of flying. The organization also works hard to preserve the history of women in aviation.

Chapter THREE

Across the Atlantic

AMELIA EARHART LOOKED FOR A JOB IN aviation. Because flying was still quite new, there were few jobs for pilots, especially female pilots. Even though she owned her plane, it was still expensive to fly and to keep in good shape. She couldn't make enough money to afford it, and eventually she had to sell the *Canary.*

In 1924, Earhart bought a car. Her mother and father had just divorced. Earhart drove her mother from California to Boston. In Boston, Earhart couldn't settle down. She went back to school for a

In 1924, Earhart and her mother drove all the way from California to Boston, Massachusetts.

while and worked at many different jobs. Finally, she settled in a job as a social worker at Denison House. Her job was to teach English to immigrants. She enjoyed this work.

Earhart continued flying when she could. She was becoming known as a very good pilot. Then, in April 1927, she received an important phone call. She was asked to be the first woman passenger to fly across the Atlantic Ocean. George Palmer Putnam selected her for this flight. He had already published several pieces about the famous aviator Charles Lindbergh. Putnam thought the story of a woman crossing the Atlantic by air would sell books. But this was a dangerous flight, and he knew he needed an adventurous woman who loved to fly. Many people had died attempting to cross the Atlantic. Earhart was not afraid. She loved a good challenge, and this would be one of her greatest adventures of all.

The plane was called the *Friendship.* Wilmer Stultz was the pilot, and Lou Gordon

Charles Lindbergh was the first person to fly an airplane across the Atlantic Ocean.

▶ Earhart wrote the book *20 Hrs. 40 Min.* based on the notes she took during her famous first flight across the Atlantic Ocean.

Earhart, Stultz, and Gordon participate in a parade held in their honor.

was the plane's mechanic. The *Friendship* took off from Boston on June 3, 1928. Earhart took notes during the flight. She would use these notes to write a book when she returned home. The plane made one stop, in Newfoundland. The crew had to stay there for two weeks because of bad weather. Finally, on June 17, they took off on their flight across the Atlantic. They landed 20 hours and 40 minutes later, at Burry Port in southern Wales. Earhart became famous as the first woman to cross the Atlantic Ocean in an airplane.

When she returned to the United States, Earhart's life changed. Parades were held in her honor. She had job offers from many businesses. People wanted to hear her give speeches. Earhart decided to focus on work that would convince people—especially women—that it was safe to fly and that it was possible to become a pilot.

Earhart and Putnam became good friends. In 1931, she married him at his mother's home. It was a very small, quiet wedding. Earhart treasured her independence and made sure that Putnam understood that she was going to continue working and flying.

Earhart continued to add to her accomplishments in aviation. She set the women's speed record of 181 miles (291 km) per hour. She flew the first autogiro—a helicopter-type airplane—and set its **altitude** record of 18,415 feet (5,613 m). Earhart was also the first woman to make a solo round-trip flight across the United States. But she knew that she wanted to do something even bigger. She was not content with being known as the first woman passenger on a flight across the Atlantic. She set her sights on becoming the first woman to fly solo across the Atlantic!

No one had flown across the Atlantic alone since Lindbergh's famous flight of 1927. On May 20, 1932, Earhart took off from Harbour Grace, Newfoundland. The flight was not easy. Some of her flight **instruments**

Amelia Earhart and George Palmer Putnam shortly after their wedding

failed. The wings iced up. Fuel began leaking. Earhart landed the plane as soon as she saw land. She was in Northern Ireland. She had made it in record time—14 hours, 56 minutes!

There were huge celebrations for Earhart. She met famous people in Great Britain, Belgium, and Italy. U.S. president Herbert Hoover presented her with the National Geographic Society's Gold Medal. She was also awarded the Distinguished Flying Cross and received a National Aeronautical Association Honorary Membership.

President Herbert Hoover presents Earhart with the National Geographic Society's Gold Medal.

Earhart was even more famous and well respected than before. But she was not interested in being famous. She was interested in proving to the world that aviation was important for society.

22

GEORGE PALMER PUTNAM WAS A MEMBER OF the family that owned G. P. Putnam's Sons publishing company. He published many books and was especially interested in books about exploration and adventure. He had published books about Charles Lindbergh and his famous first solo flight across the Atlantic Ocean. He knew that if a woman were to cross the Atlantic by plane, it would make a great story. He chose Amelia Earhart to be the first woman passenger to cross the Atlantic. From that moment on, he was an important part of her life.

Putnam was married to Dorothy Binney Putnam. That marriage ended in December 1929. By then, he was working closely with Earhart. He had published her book, *20 Hrs. 40 Min.,* and arranged many public appearances for her. They became good friends.

Eventually, Putnam asked Earhart to marry him. At first, she said no. She had seen her parents' unhappy marriage and was not sure about marriage for herself. Finally, she said yes. They were married on February 7, 1931. The wedding took place in Noank, Connecticut, at the home of Putnam's mother.

Amelia Earhart kept her own last name and did not change it to Putnam. She also had an agreement with Putnam that being his wife would not keep her from flying. Putnam worked closely with Earhart as she continued her aviation career.

In 1939, two years after Earhart disappeared during a flight, Putnam wrote about his beloved wife. The title of this biography is *Soaring Wings* and it is his tribute to Amelia Earhart.

A Big Adventure, A Big Mystery

AMELIA EARHART CONTINUED FLYING AND setting records. In 1932, she set the women's record for flying from one coast of the United States to the other. One year later, she broke that record and set a new one. In 1935, she became the first person to fly solo from Honolulu, Hawaii, to Oakland, California, and from Los Angeles, California, to Mexico City, Mexico.

Earhart took a job at Purdue University in Lafayette, Indiana. She helped young women decide on careers and did research on flying. She also went into the charter-airline business. Earhart's work at Purdue impressed many people. A group formed an organization called the Amelia Earhart Fund for Aeronautical Research. In 1936, on Earhart's

39th birthday, the organization gave her a plane for research. It was the most advanced plane in the world for nonmilitary use. She referred to the shiny Lockheed Electra as her "flying laboratory." Earhart wanted to take the Electra around the world. If she was successful, she would become the first woman to fly around the world. Earhart was not interested in the fame. She saw it as an opportunity to do more research for aviation.

Amelia Earhart and Fred Noonan go over maps of the Pacific Ocean before their final flight.

It took many people to plan this flight. Countries around the world where Earhart needed to stop were involved. Oil companies were prepared to provide fuel around the world. Even President Franklin Delano Roosevelt was involved. The U.S. Navy would have ships in the Pacific Ocean to help her.

On June 1, 1937, after many months of preparation, Earhart took off on her flight. She was not alone. With her was a man

Interesting Fact

▸ Earhart was the first woman to be awarded the Distinguished Flying Cross.

Earhart started designing women's clothes in 1932. Her first outfit was a flying suit for women pilots. It was advertised in *Vogue* magazine.

named Fred Noonan. He was a **navigator.** He would help her know where the plane was flying and where they were supposed to land.

For several weeks, the flight went as planned, with only minor problems. Several repairs had to be made at each stop, and storms slowed them down.

Finally, on July 2, 1937, Earhart and Noonan took off from Lae, Papua New Guinea. It was almost the end of the trip. Earhart hoped to be home in two more days. But this was a dangerous part of the flight. They had to land on Howland Island, a very tiny island in the middle of the Pacific Ocean.

People on Howland Island preparing for Earhart's arrival.

There would be just enough fuel to make the distance. A Navy ship was positioned in the water near the island. The ship received a radio message from Earhart that her plane was close by and they were looking for the island. Earhart and Noonan couldn't see it.

Later, the ship again got a message from Earhart. She said they were still searching for the island. That was the last communication from Earhart. Her plane never landed on Howland Island. Earhart, Noonan, and the plane had disappeared.

President Roosevelt ordered a huge sea and air search for Earhart. Navy planes and ships searched the waters and the islands of the Pacific. People everywhere wanted to help. The search continued for almost a month. No clues were found. Earhart, Noonan, and the Lockheed Electra were lost at sea.

Interesting Fact

▶ Before leaving on their around-the-world flight, Fred Noonan said of Earhart, "Amelia is a grand person for such a trip. She is the only woman flyer I would care to make such an expedition with."

▶ TIGHAR is a group that has spent years studying information about Earhart's disappearance. TIGHAR stands for **T**he **I**nternational **G**roup for **H**istoric **A**ircraft **R**ecovery.

Nauticos is another group that has tried locating Earhart's plane. This is the same group that filmed the wreckage of the *Titanic*.

Earhart's disappearance has remained a mystery for more than 50 years. Her plane has never been found. Several search efforts have tried, but failed.

Throughout her life, Amelia Earhart looked for challenge and loved adventure. She worked tirelessly to show women that they could be successful in many careers. Her accomplishments in aviation left an impact on the American people and society. Her courage gave strength to both men and women. She will never be forgotten.

Amelia Earhart's courage and love of adventure continue to be an inspiration to many people today.

1897   1921   1937

1897   Amelia Earhart is born on July 24 in Atchison, Kansas.

1916   Earhart enters Ogontz School in Pennsylvania.

1918   Earhart takes a job as a nurse's aide at Spadina Military Hospital in Toronto, Canada.

1919   After returning to the United States, Earhart begins premedical studies at Columbia University in New York.

1920   Earhart attends an air show and takes her first airplane ride.

1921   Earhart begins flying lessons.

1922   Earhart purchases the *Canary*, her first airplane, with financial help from her mother and sister. On October 22, she sets her first flight record, flying at an altitude of 14,000 feet (4,267 m).

1926   Earhart takes a job as a social worker at Denison House in Boston, Massachusetts.

1928   Earhart becomes the first woman passenger to fly across the Atlantic Ocean.

1929   The Ninety-Nines, an organization of female aviators, is started by Earhart and 98 other woman pilots.

1931   Earhart and George Palmer Putnam are married on February 7.

1932   Earhart becomes the first woman to fly solo across the Atlantic and is awarded the National Geographic Society's Gold Medal and the Distinguished Flying Cross. Later that year, she sets the women's coast-to-coast speed record in a flight from Los Angeles, California, to Newark, New Jersey.

1933   Earhart breaks her Los Angeles to Newark speed record.

1935   Earhart becomes the first pilot to fly alone from Honolulu, Hawaii, to Oakland, California. She also becomes the first pilot to fly alone from Los Angeles, California, to Mexico City, Mexico, and from Mexico City to Newark, New Jersey. In September, she begins working as a career consultant at Purdue University in Indiana.

1937   On June 1, Earhart takes off for an around-the-world flight with navigator Fred Noonan. The plane disappears on July 3 in the South Pacific. Earhart, Noonan, and the plane are never found.

aerospace (AIR-oh-spayss)
The atmosphere surrounding Earth and the space beyond it are referred to as aerospace. The Ninety-Nines is an organization of women involved in aviation and the study of aerospace.

alcoholism (AL-kuh-hol-iz-um)
Alcoholism is a sickness in which a person is addicted to drinking alcohol. Amelia Earhart's father suffered from alcoholism.

altitude (AL-tih-tood)
Altitude is the measurement of how high something is above the ground. Earhart set many altitude records during her flying career.

aviation (ay-vee-AY-shun)
Aviation is the science of designing aircraft or the act of flying them. Earhart was fascinated by aviation.

derby (DUR-bee)
A derby is a race. Amelia Earhart raced her airplane in the Women's Air Derby.

instruments (IN-struh-ments)
Instruments are tools that help you perform a task. The plane's flight instruments helped Earhart fly safely in bad weather.

mechanical (meh-KAN-ih-kull)
If something is mechanical, it is related to machinery. Earhart liked to build mechanical things.

navigator (NAV-uh-gate-er)
A navigator is the person who figures out the position of an aircraft or a ship and makes sure that it stays on course. Fred Noonan was the navigator for Earhart's trip around the world.

premedical (pree-MED-ih-kull)
Premedical refers to a course of study required before entering medical school. Amelia Earhart began her premedical studies at Columbia University in New York.

For Further INFORMATION

Web Sites

Visit our homepage for lots of links about Amelia Earhart:
http://www.childsworld.com/links.html

Note to Parents, Teachers, and Librarians:
We routinely verify our Web links to make sure they're safe,
active sites—so encourage your readers to check them out!

Books

Jerome, Kate Boehm, and David Cain (illustrator). *Who Was Amelia Earhart?*
New York: Grosset and Dunlap, 2002.

Szabo, Corinne. *Sky Pioneer: A Photobiography of Amelia Earhart.* Washington,
D.C.: National Geographic Society, 1997.

Places to Visit or Contact

The Ninety-Nines, Inc. International Headquarters
To write for more information on the history of women in aviation and the programs
offered by the Ninety-Nines
7100 Terminal Drive, Box 965
Oklahoma City, OK 73159-0965
405/685-7969

Amelia Earhart Birthplace Museum
To visit the house where Amelia Earhart was born and to learn more about her life
and adventures
223 North Terrace Street
Atchison, KS 66002
913/367-4217

Index

About the Author

CYNTHIA KLINGEL HAS WORKED AS A HIGH SCHOOL English teacher and an elementary school teacher. She is currently the curriculum director for a Minnesota school district. Cynthia Klingel lives with her family in Mankato, Minnesota.